PHYSICIAN'S BOOK OF

WEALTH SECRETS

Alternative-Based Investing For Financial Independence

THOMAS BLACK, MD MBA

PUBLISHED IN THE UNITED STATES OF AMERICA

Second Edition

Disclaimer

Nothing in this book shall be construed as an offer for investment in Black-Bridge Financial, LLC. Solicitations for investments will only be made through a Private Placement Memorandum provided by the company to potential investors for such purposes.

The information in this book is solely for providing information about the Company's business model and investment strategies. The information contained herein is the sole property of the Company and may not be copied or reproduced without the Company's express written consent. While the information in this presentation has been compiled from sources we believe to be reliable, neither the Company nor its representatives make any representations or warranties regarding the accuracy or completeness contained herein. All financial information in this book is provided for reference only and is based on assumptions relating to the general economy, market conditions, and other factors beyond the Company's control.

Statements included in this presentation address activities, events, or developments that the Company anticipates will or may occur in the future. These statements are based on certain assumptions and analyses made by the Company considering its experience and perception of historical trends, current conditions, and expected future developments. However, whether actual results will conform with these expectations is subject to several risks and uncertainties, many of which are beyond the control of the Company, including but not limited to risks endemic to real estate investing, oil and gas investing, variations in residential housing demand, general business cycles, interest rate changes, and commodity prices. Thus, these cautionary statements qualify all the forward-looking statements in this book.

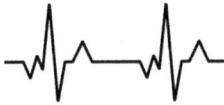

For all those who sacrifice nights, weekends, holidays, and precious time with family in the service of healthcare to others.

TABLE OF CONTENTS

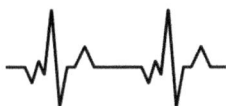

FOREWORD

The Physician's Book of Wealth Secrets proposes a simple data-driven operating system for creating wealth while practicing medicine. Dr. Thomas Black, MD MBA developed the operating system, which has been at the forefront of creating alternative action-based investing and education platforms.

Regardless of your current financial situation, subspecialty, or practice, you can become "wealthy." Most people in the U.S. consider doctors wealthy. If you are reading this, you likely know this to be false. Over the past several decades, the fleecing of the profession has led to flat incomes and increased expenses despite more demand. We have used ineffective medical records systems built only for corporate/owner revenue and have worked significantly more extended hours. Physician burnout is rampant. The definition of wealth needs to change. Wealth should be defined as "the ability to leave your profession or practice when you want, with a cash flow that continues without having to labor for it." Wealth and *financial freedom* should be a safety net that allows physicians who have sacrificed years and the time value of money to continue to practice whether they choose to or not.

This book is a collection of years of experience including huge successes and some failures. It aims to improve the financial health of doctors and those in the healthcare industry who sacrifice so much. If you are not familiar with his story, Tom was a less-than-stellar student in high school and thus joined the military to advance his education. He was fortunate to find a fire within and a thirst for knowledge that informed his future. A few life incidents led him into the medical profession, a tall order for a guy who could not go to college right out of high school. Tom was accepted into medical school and graduated from Alpha Omega Alpha with honors in research, giving him the choice of his career path. He was passionate about setting and achieving goals, but, like most professionals, he wondered what was next as he entered clinical practice.

Early in his practice, Tom failed to grasp that becoming a doctor was not his end game. His intense drive through medical school and his practice caused him to lose sight of setting life goals. Disappointment soon set in—the things that made him truly happy were not happening, and he began to feel a touch helpless.

After years of studying and taking medical licensing exams, Tom began to recognize his mistake in thinking his finances would automatically fall into place. He saw that private companies were increasingly leveraging the profession and felt that becoming a physician may have been a career mistake, despite his love for his work and helping others. Whereas he enjoyed the mental challenge and was inspired in his practice, money always became a foundational issue representing all the energy and time expended. He realized that working nights, weekends, and holidays differed from the future he wanted for himself and his family. He wanted freedom, not just economic security. He wanted the power of choice only derived through *ownership and equity*.

That's when Tom's entrepreneurial drive kicked in. By discovering alternative investing and helping other physicians start the investment process, Tom found he could mesh his professional career and investment passion, thereby gaining a foothold on the path to financial freedom—his ultimate goal. Ironically, the companies leveraging healthcare became the blueprint for salvation.

If you're holding this book, you likely realize that earning wages and savings will be inadequate for the quality of retirement you want. You will need an active investment strategy that leads to more cash flow. You will need not only a perpetual engine that will generate more income than what you might traditionally receive through mutual funds or IRA investments, but a consistent tax strategy that allows you to keep more of your hard-earned income.

This book is organized into the four stages of investment that will help you approach financial freedom:

1. Assessment: Your Net Worth & Your Terminal Value Objective
2. Evaluate & Strategize: Understanding the Paths
3. Time to Dive In: Creating Your Path Forward
4. Leveraging Tax: My Chosen Direction

PHYSICIAN'S BOOK OF

WEALTH SECRETS

Alternative-Based Investing For Financial Independence

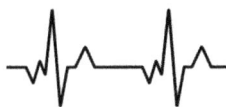

TALK ONE

ASSESSMENT: YOUR NET WORTH &
YOUR TERMINAL VALUE OBJECTIVE

MOTIVATION

Years ago, I was heading to my son's little league game on a Saturday morning. I was still in scrubs after an ugly 12-hour shift in the emergency department. My wife needed backup, handling four kids under five-years-old. Upon seeing me at the game, my shocked kids innocently asked why I was there. Wasn't there somewhere else I was supposed to be? This was not the first time the kids had questioned my presence. It had become all too routine. But this was the stark realization—I was not often present. I was missing critical moments in their childhoods.

The austere quality of life and the long residency hours were sacrifice enough. I wondered, "Is this what life is supposed to be?" After twelve years of school, being a doctor was everything I had worked for. Yet my kids were wondering why I was at a game on a Saturday morning. It was apparent that what I was doing wouldn't work long-term. Retirement was too far in the future, while my family was here and now, and I needed to seriously assess my life, my net worth, and how to manage things differently.

This talk is about that wake-up call. You've either had it, or it is coming, and you need to be ready to interpret what it means.

ASSESSMENT

A marathon starts with a single step in the right direction. In this section, we will define the start of the journey and, more importantly, the goals and objectives that must be created. Not having a goal leads to inefficiency. Life may be about the journey, but with no goal, there is no destination. Having a goal or destination only makes the journey that much more enjoyable, and it also makes it faster. A goal can always be changed along the way, forging a new path and destination.

The journey is defined as increasing your net worth, and the destination is a Terminal Value Objective—the accumulative wealth needed to maintain your desired lifestyle.

We have all observed that many physicians fall into the high-cash-flow/high-salary position but not the high-net-worth category. In other words, when a physician stops working, the cash flow slows or stops.

This section will discuss net worth, cash flow, and the ultimate goal: the Terminal Value Objective.

As we have been taught throughout our medical training, care begins with a subjective and objective assessment and then moves to a plan. This process is no different.

STEP 1 - PERFORM A SUBJECTIVE LIFE CHECK

Here, we ask, "Where do I want to be?" We encourage everyone at this stage to make a list and take stock; consider your desired lifestyle. What does happiness look like to you?

- Where do I want to live?
- Do I want a second home?
- What type of house would I like to own?
- At what age do I want to stop working?
- Where do I want to take my vacations?

- What hobbies would I enjoy if money was no object?

Any format will work. You might define your goal in five-year increments, annual earnings, or future net worth. There is no right or wrong way to contemplate what happiness looks like. But writing it down is the first step in the process. This is the time to dream and to create a few statements that define your goal.

STEP 2 - CONDUCT A THOROUGH NET-WORTH ASSESSMENT

The first step was subjective; this step is objective. It is relatively straightforward, and much information is available in publications and websites on assessing your current financial status. Simply put, your net worth is equal to your assets minus your liabilities. A quick internet search for a net worth spreadsheet or calculator will reveal many sources to use and download.

This assessment is not intended to generate good or bad feelings or to give the sensation of invincibility or doom. A strategy can only be drafted or pursued by first understanding the baseline. This objective exercise provides that baseline and will be a dynamic document for use in the future. Most physicians are surprised after taking stock of their current net worth—they don't realize the impact that living a physician lifestyle and managing medical school debt has had on current value.

Understanding your current net worth will help tremendously as we proceed through the next several steps in this book.

STEP 3 - CALCULATE THE "GAP" BETWEEN YOUR CURRENT NET WORTH AND YOUR TERMINAL VALUE OBJECTIVE

Understanding the difference between your current and retirement net worth is the ultimate objective of all financial planners, and there are many ways to accomplish this. We aim to focus on the Terminal Value Objective, the confluence of net worth, and your Life Check Assessment. Your goal might be a particular net worth at a certain age or retirement at a certain age.

The Terminal Value Objective is a dollar amount that equates to financial freedom or the ability to live a particular lifestyle by a certain age. For many physicians, this means an income not tied to earned income from a sole source or practice that requires untenable work hours.

Your Terminal Value Objective will drive your planning as you move through this process.

SECRETS

- Taking the time to do a life check seems almost trivial, but determining a goal and a desired lifestyle is critical. Imagine a runner signing up for a marathon and accepting that they will stop running when they want, giving no thought to the finish line. Everyone needs a goal.
- Only through acknowledging your current net worth and contemplating a better future can a meaningful strategy for change be created.
- Each person's Terminal Value Objective and goal will change often. Nevertheless, determining and evaluating your Terminal Value Objective at the outset is critical to help build a strategy that works for you.

CHECKLIST

- ☐ Conduct a life check to create a vision of the future in the language that makes sense to you.
- ☐ Calculate your current net worth.
- ☐ Calculate the gap between your current net worth and the cost of your future vision. (This is critical to understanding

the Terminal Value Objective.)

FINAL THOUGHT

We are valued but increasingly seen as a commodity.

As physicians, we are highly trained individuals in the healthcare world. Years of hard work and sacrifice have placed us in the position to deliver invaluable healthcare.

But what has happened to our profession in the last few decades? We have been leveraged into practices owned by other entities. We no longer make all decisions based on our training and evidence-based science. The government has mandated reimbursements based on how we document our work and the tests we order. Corporations and hospital systems are paying physicians an hourly wage predicated on "fair market value."

Where is the autonomy that ruled our profession? Red tape and bureaucracy have dominated the field. So, how do we take control of our destiny and create an environment of freedom? The answer is to change our financial mindset.

Medicine is now about money and revenue. This may sound harsh, but once accepted, a much clearer perspective appears. Medical administration, billing, and the machinations of our corporate parents are easier to understand once we understand and accept the rules of the game. Our success is hinged upon first realizing that we are a leveraged commodity. Right or wrong, this is reality, and until the pendulum swings in the opposite direction, understanding the field is important for self-preservation.

This book aims to rebalance the perspective and allow physicians to build equity in themselves. We need a mindset of leverage, and we should learn to use our skills and education to help ourselves and, ultimately, our relationships with others.

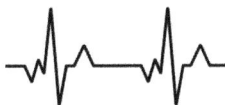

TALK TWO

Doesn't it seem that someone is always trying to sell us something? Even early on in medical school, battalions of drug reps tried to peddle the latest and greatest cure-all for diseases. The reps always seemed very knowledgeable and confident in the specific drug and area of care, but couldn't speak to the patient's overall needs. Knowing a drug's side effects, benefits, and organic makeup is impressive, but that was where the drug rep's knowledge ended.

The drug reps' sector-specific knowledge and product confidence is paralleled in the financial industry. A rep pushes a product and is incentivized to use their solution for a particular use, just like a financial advisor is incentivized to use certain investment products for specific strategies. Regardless of good intentions, a bias remains that alters the advisor's recommendations, just as it does in our practices. For example, generic drugs that don't generate as much profit are treated just like low-margin investment vehicles, which usually appear in the small print when presented by some financial advisors.

WHERE DO YOU GET YOUR ADVICE?

Financial advisors exist because individuals often limit themselves when managing their finances. There is inertia against learning anything beyond what doctors hear on CNBC about financial management.

Let's talk about financial advisors. Are they wealthy, or is their net worth less than that of their average client? How have they made their money? Are they just taking fees? We submit that financial advising is a highly lucrative industry full of many types of people with different agendas. We are not suggesting they are bad people. Just be aware of their motivations; statistically speaking, only a few are exclusively for the client.

WHAT'S WRONG WITH PAYING FOR ADVICE?

Nothing, if there is a return on the investment. Gaining financial planning and tax reduction knowledge and then pursuing a growth strategy can significantly improve the returns. Paying for the advice and excessive fees can destroy two-thirds of a portfolio. In his epic *Unshakeable*, Tony Robbins deftly explained it: "Let's assume the stock market gives a 7% return over 50 years, and because of the power of compounding, each dollar goes up to 30. But the fund charges you about 2% per year in costs, which drops your average returns to 5%. At that rate, you get $10 versus $30. You placed 100% of the capital, took 100% of the risk, and got 33% of the return!" Minimizing fees and understanding the investments and tax implications can save years and hundreds of thousands of dollars in a portfolio.

Remember, financial advisors have only an upside; they experience no downside risk with your investment dollars.

A WORD ABOUT RISK

Financial advisors will assess your risk profile when developing your investment strategy. Conservative strategies will drive safe returns for you and your advisor relationship. High-risk strategies can deliver profit in the portfolio, but this leads to tension with the advisor during turbulent markets. An underscoring theme has also focused on risk perception.

This book views the pursuit of and equity ownership in assets as the way to combat risk. Rather than focusing on the strict risk parameters above, focus on the perception of risk and how the risk-averse mindset can do more harm than good. It sounds counterintuitive, but a defensive strategy only works sometimes. We believe it's true that "you cannot save your way to wealth," and generating wealth in medicine should not be taboo. Generating wealth and income beyond a paycheck should be the salvation for physicians and the source of happiness in our practice.

MY CASE AGAINST MUTUAL FUNDS AS A MAJOR PATHWAY

The most touted path to financial freedom is its focus on stocks and mutual funds. Unless an investor was fortunate or insightful enough to have bought the right amount of Amazon™, Google™, and Facebook™ stocks at the right time, chances are their investments are in mutual funds. From our perspective, picking stocks has too many variables. We have no transparency in how the company is run or how business decisions are made. And, as busy physicians, we don't have the time needed to research or track all the companies that seem like a good bet.

We are not suggesting that all stocks or mutual funds are bad investments, but the vast volume of offerings and the knowledge required to pick and track make it challenging to leverage large returns without significant risk. There are too many stories about stock tips going bad.

So, what is the magic formula for choosing a mutual fund? There are roughly 9,500 mutual funds, **significantly more than**

twice the number of publicly traded companies. Why so many? Because it's crazy-lucrative for Wall Street. Well-meaning advisors are out there, but how do you decipher who they are truly working for? Even those advisors with the best intentions are still working within a system designed to make money.

How are mutual funds managed? Again, in Tony Robbins' *Unshakeable*, he explains it well:

"When fund managers trade in and out of companies, there are ample opportunities for mistakes. Humans are prone to errors, and trading companies in the portfolio leads to more decisions. Not only decisions of when to sell a position but how much and which ones? The more decisions that are faced, the more chances for error.

To make matters worse, all the trading gets expensive. Every time a fund trades in and out of a stock, the firm charges a commission to execute the transaction. Like a casino, the house gets paid every time a move is made. The house never loses. Also, you'll have to pay the capital gains tax when a stock goes up. Even if you are not selling your share at the time, these gains are passed through to the fund in real time, increasing cost. For investors in a managed fund, all these changes eat away at your profits, but they still make money on those funds being utilized. After all these fees and taxes, the value must be significant enough for the fund to win."

What is the fund rating myth? Unfortunately, many people fall into the trap of buying top-rated funds without realizing that they are buying what's "hot." Nobody wants to buy 1-and-2-star funds. Investors want to own 4-and-5-star products. But the 4-and-5-star products have performed well *recently*; they are not necessarily the funds that have performed well *historically*! Consistently buying into high-rated funds will likely lead to a portfolio's underperformance.

There is another problem that few amateur fund researchers anticipate: today's performers are tomorrow's losers. *The Wall Street Journal* published a well-researched article examining what happened to all top-performing funds (funds that received a 5-star rating from Morningstar) over ten years. What did they discover? Of the 248 mutual funds, only *four* kept their 5-star rating, and the remaining 244 reverted to mediocrity. What does this all mean? Money is made with opportunity in the future. We often pay for a Ferrari™ that quickly turns into a Honda™ in the market. **See money with your mind**.

THE STRATEGY

Your Terminal Value Objective is the goal. There are many ways to get there, and many advisors are willing to point the way. The purpose of this section is to encourage you to evaluate the methods and determine a strategy that will deliver your financial freedom. This will take some work.

STARTING POINTS

Active vs. Passive (Residual) Income

Active income is likely the only income most people know. Wake up, go to work, come home, cash a check. Hours worked x your wage = active income.

Passive income, sometimes called residual income, results from cash flow received regularly and requires minimal to no effort by the recipient to grow or maintain. Examples of passive income include rental income, oil and gas, royalties, and any business activities in which the earner does not materially participate during the year. As the great Warren Buffet sums up, "If you don't find a way to make money while you sleep, you will work until you die."

Earning vs. Equity

Most advice centers around this fundamental concept. Once out of residency, physicians are likely in a unique period of their career where they can earn a decent salary. These earnings, whether as a W2 employee or a 1099 contractor, are the return for exerting skills and knowledge. When a physician stops exerting skills or expertise, the earnings also stop. Your ability to generate income is your greatest strength right now. So, what you do with that income is critical.

The absolute key is ownership of the asset. There are various types of equity, but equity typically refers to shareholder equity, which represents the amount of money that would be returned to a company's shareholders if all the assets were liquidated—if all the company's debt was paid off. We can think of equity as a degree of ownership in any asset after subtracting all debts associated with that asset.

This is key: Earnings and active income are essential—after all, most of us need to work and earn income to survive today. The ideal platform is founded on the simple principle that your Terminal Value Objective is driven by *revenue* generated by distributions from the equity in the asset. Under most earning circumstances, passive income through equity accelerates the path to financial freedom.

There are hundreds of books, with more coming every month, on how to create an effective investment strategy. Creating this strategy will take time and some reflection. You must determine how to build equity and generate income while maximizing your salary-earning potential. With this method, you will always put as much of your income as you can spare into assets that generate a return. Alternative asset investments that generate distributions or passive income (ie. real estate, oil and gas, private equity, private credit, and venture capital) have consistently been effective at generating wealth in numerous economic environments.

Tax: You Must Learn to See Things Differently

Change the facts of your financial life—the limiting beliefs that handcuff your effort to excel—and you'll begin to experience a new, expansive relationship with money. The change starts when you embrace the tax code. Even in medical school, I knew I would have a significant tax burden once out of training. It is painful to think about working free of charge for the Internal Revenue Service for four months every year with a tax rate of at least 37 percent. **The average doctor pays over 50 percent of their annual income** when combining all the various taxing forms (sales, payroll, estate, property, income).

I could go on for hours about this topic; I have. My second book, *The Tax Cure: Changing the Facts of Your Financial Life to Create True Wealth and Peace of Mind*, is available on Amazon. However, the first step in this *Physician's Book of Wealth Secrets* is awareness. Tax can be a map to accelerated success. We will touch on this more in Talk #4.

How to Develop Your Strategy

Passive income takes some time to develop. Most physicians have income to start, so let's focus on that.

Take the first step. Attend a lecture, connect with a capital management firm, or invest in an income-generating asset. There is no prescribed starting point. Just get in the game. Consider this your tuition for learning. The goal is to gain comfort and build on the experience. It is a simple process that is slow and takes time and effort. As physicians, we've been tested to our mental capacity, and creating wealth is just addition and subtraction, no more complicated than dosing a pediatric prescription. Once the first deal is tackled, subsequent deals will be more straightforward. As each asset begins to create cash flow, repeat the process when income allows.

SECRETS

- Many investment sources present solutions that work against existing strategies in your portfolio by cannibalizing returns with offsetting strategies. Therefore, having a consistent strategy tied to your Terminal Value Objective is critical.
- Building your own operating system or investment strategy is the best way to manage the advice and guidance you will get from countless sources.
- The strategy focuses on reaching your Terminal Value Objective while maximizing your current income and diverting as much as possible into equity or a passive income strategy.
- Alternative or hard assets have numerous advantages over other investment vehicles and should be strongly considered as supplemental to your strategy.
- Learn to love taxes. This is your single largest expense every year, but with planning, it could be your biggest savings. Imagine reinvesting that six-figure bill back into your investing machine every year!

CHECKLIST

- ☐ Reach out to an investment professional and understand their strategy for success.
- ☐ Partner with another physician who is investing in alternative assets.
- ☐ Plan your first investment to test the waters.

FINAL THOUGHT

If you want to know the focus of those in the C-suite, it's procedures and revenue. Make no mistake: healthcare is a business, pure and simple. How can we use this to our advantage in everyday practice? We are the patient's advocate. The more you learn about money and the mindset of wealthy business owners and executives, the more you can recognize their maneuvers. If you know how your opponent plays chess and can predict their next move, you can develop a winning strategy. Healthcare business practices can be summed up as increasing revenue while decreasing expenses and, yes, taking care of patients.

Facility fees and inpatient revenue account for most of the income to sustain operations, but you can't bill without having doctors! We are the reason that the healthcare industry exists. Fees drive millions to the bottom line, but these millions are not necessarily shared with the givers of care or used to fund the safety net of the operation. Our work and, therefore, our liability serves to generate profits. Unfortunately, laws preclude physician equity in most cases. The Stark Law, for example, changes the landscape of physician ownership in healthcare ventures. Passed in 1990, the Stark Law essentially stopped any new development of healthcare ventures for doctors to be awarded equity. Seen as a conflict of interest, Congress enacted rules for physicians to no longer own hospital positions. They could continue as a part of an existing group; however, this significantly reduced the future expansion or development of the entities. This was seen as the death of physician entrepreneurship. Yet, insurance companies are allowed to own drug companies. Welcome to the monopolization of healthcare. The only successful strategy is to play on the field and learn the rules so that we play smarter.

The time for strategy is now.

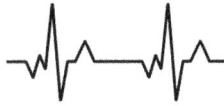

TALK THREE

TIME TO DIVE IN: CREATING YOUR PATH FORWARD

The strategies and thought processes we've discussed so far were launched in 2008. At the time, I had a home that was worth less than what I paid for it. I bought a few books on taxation and real estate and became enamored with finance and cash flow. When I left residency, selling my upside-down home was not an option. I wanted the cash flow, even if only a few dollars! Then opportunity knocked. I found an incoming resident who needed a place to live and negotiated a lease for three years of training!

After settling into my first real post-residency job, I began to buy foreclosure homes to rehab and lease for cash flow. This was the awakening of my financial education and resulting success. I was consumed with how I could create a "cash flow" machine. This process was forged on calculating the equity needed to generate enough cash to reduce my workload by one monthly shift. It was an absolute motivator to continue learning and leveraging the machine I began to build. Soon, one shift a month became two, then a week a month, and the process continued until I reached a point where I could leave medicine entirely if I chose. A funny thing happened, though. All the frustration and anxiety changed. Through all the work, a new perspective emerged, and I began to enjoy working. Did all of this occur overnight? Absolutely not. It took work and sacrifice, but it is attainable and more straightforward than the many mountains each of us has climbed, getting through the gauntlet of medical training and licensure. It is 100% achievable if you decide mentally to make the change.

This section discusses building the machine to generate more wealth, eventually leading to your Terminal Value Objective.

THE FIRST STEP

As I did with an upside-down house, the action starts with jumping in—which you must do quickly. Now is not the time to wait for all the answers; it is the time to act.

You will need to do more than simply trade time for money to achieve your goal. Design your life in reverse, starting with your goal and working backward until you reach the present day. What will it take *now* to get *there*? Most wealthy people in this country receive 70% of their income from investments and less than 30% from wages as an employee. In contrast, middle-income earners and physicians receive 80% of their income from wages and less than 20% from investment income. If your money comes from a job, you are likely not on the path to financial freedom.

BUILDING YOUR CASH FLOW MACHINE

The action plan is simple: Create the cash flow machine. Invest in that machine. When the machine starts paying dividends or generates cash from the liquidation of an asset, re-invest that money or place it in another asset class that creates even more cash. It's not instantaneous, but it is fruitful and will get you to your goals. It will simply take time and patience.

How do you create a pathway to practicing medicine on your

own? Here's one way: I began investing not only in my financial education but also in my financial machine. I started buying single-family homes to rent, but then learned that my time and effort could be used to create much larger returns with the same effort by entering the world of commercial real estate and oil and gas ventures.

The first step was small. I began with income-generating properties managed by a 3rd party that I could watch over. Soon after, my assets began generating revenue independently, and I started doing small and productive developments. Whenever an asset began creating distribution, I took those earnings and I invested in other asset classes based on cash flow or tax-incentivized strategies to augment the machine's maximum output. After the foundational cash-flow machine became self-sustaining, I slowly reduced my clinical workload, using that time for more opportunities.

FORECLOSING, FLIPPING, AND LEVERAGE

Every period and environment has advantages and opportunities. It takes skill and experience to recognize, but it comes with time. Given the economic conditions when I started (remember, it was 2008), I became entrenched in foreclosure acquisitions. I considered these opportunities the perfect segue to create a portfolio. Flipping homes was a commonplace practice at the time, and this was the early stages of the flipping explosion we saw in the US, post-depression. Flipping, for me, was very short-sighted. Why would someone, especially a physician, spend inordinate hours rehabbing a home to flip when the gains would be taxed at a maximum rate? Not only was this a time-sucking exercise with speed-to-market being so critical, but the risk was much more significant than I could tolerate. It is not as easy as it looks. Long hours, dead ends, and unpredictable buyers. Then, after all this risk and work, you get taxed at the highest rate!

But on the positive side, I rehabbed these homes for rentals that I intended to hold to create not only cash flow but depreciation and appreciation. Plus, I was taking advantage of the bank, which gave me 90 to 100% of the funds since the homes were valued more than I was paying for them! This was the start of my income-generating machine.

PARTNERING

Taking the first leap is the most difficult, but it does force education and introduces the necessity for a self-guided strategy to building net worth. This process recommends that the first step is making an investment with a known partner or reputable firm with a good track record. You will find, early on, that picking the asset or product is less important than choosing the right partner. Having an excellent track record and foundation is paramount. Bad things can and will happen, but the key to a good partner is transparency and integrity when things go awry. The best lessons may lie here. No one bats 1000%, but positives always arise, even in what appear to be failures. Find these people. You either win or you learn—either is just as valuable.

Everyone looks impressive when times are great, but communication and wisdom mean everything when the chips are down. If you've ever heard someone say that being in a bad business partnership is worse than divorce, believe them! The physical and emotional toll it will take is excruciating. In summary, do your homework. People and processes matter, even if the asset looks like an incredible opportunity you can't pass up.

The more your network grows, the more opportunities you will have thrust upon you. Not all opportunities will be great, and wisdom must dictate which you pursue; however, your network drives your chances and, therefore, your net worth. The key is to create cash-flow opportunities outside the hours you work. Remember, your goal should be to generate money while you sleep.

OTHER ESSENTIAL PARTNERSHIPS

Contrary to the practice of medicine, the funny thing is that wealth is a team sport. Finding the right partners is essential for the machine to operate efficiently. Tax advisors, operational partners, management partners, insurance agents, and attorneys (both contract and tax) all play a role.

It took the team years to find the right tax partner. I went through many CPAs and firms. As the business and understanding grew, so did the need for a partner who understood our needs. As you become more sophisticated, you may outgrow your partners—and you must understand and accept this. It's a sign that the machine is growing and moving in the right direction. I have found that partners are just as important as the assets we invest in. The right asset and investment means nothing without a strategy and a team to manage it.

Physicians often make the same investment mistakes by picking the wrong partners or not investing in their relationships. Entering an investment is easy and far less important than managing the exit. The investment exit can be tricky from a tax planning perspective, and finding the right tax partner is critical. Efficient tax planning can exponentially grow your machine to create cash flow. This "practice" of finding the right partner holds for your entire team. When you find the right partner, create value for them. Leverage works both ways. You may find that, depending on your style, your partners may outgrow you in their business model too!

SECRETS

- As a physician with board certification, you realize that you are economically safe concerning income. You can always treat people well and you know you won't be destitute. Don't let this lull you into a false sense of security. Your most extensive resource today is your ability to earn a salary. But if you want out someday, you must build a machine to generate enough cash to reach your Terminal Value Objective.

- Building the Machine should start with something small, but it must start with something. Buy something, own something. Start small.

- Partner with a reputable capital management firm to test the waters and see how returns are generated.

- Growing your wealth is a team activity. Partner with professionals you trust to continue to build your machine.

CHECKLIST

- ☐ You need a team to accelerate growth. Over the next 30 days, schedule a meeting with someone who is further along financially than you. Hear what they have to say.

- ☐ Find a tax advisor, not just an accountant, who understands and is willing to be creative. Take your time to select the right advisor. Like physicians, not all accountants are the same. Find someone who is an expert aligned with your investment goals and strategy and who understands the benefits of real estate investing. *A good reason for forming a real estate LLC is the write-offs. You can't do that with a W-2 or even through owning a practice.*

- ☐ Connect with reputable people and try to invest in your first venture, even if it is small.

FINAL THOUGHT

Alternative Investments "AKA Alternatives" and the PPM:
The Secret Weapon Against Wall Street

While a partner in what seemed to be the last private democratic EM practice in East Texas, I began developing and building apartment complexes on the side and learning oil and gas operations. I often left the ER late in the morning and parked on the property while it was under construction, in awe of what was being created. From here, I would drive by the drilling rigs or pumps of my oil and gas well partnerships. I found it fascinating that money was being created with my mind rather than from the hours I worked at the hospital. I realize this sounds crazy, but it didn't feel like work. I was passionate about creating something tangible and found fulfillment in something outside my career. The side job distraction helped during the times that I was feeling burned out in the ED. This is not to say your path would be the same as mine; it is only that doing something different can change your perspective. A new income stream changed my thoughts about earning, and I strived to create money with my mind rather than working hourly for it. There are endless ways to generate cash and wealth, and it all starts with how you view your situation and the world around you.

Once successful in several ventures, colleagues and acquaintances began asking how they could get involved and invest. I had no idea. I was now versed in alternative asset investing and operations, the primary legal entities, and management. However, I had yet to learn how to create a group that could see the vision and share in the profits while investing and owning a position in the deal. I was in East Texas then and had been speaking with attorneys about creating a document that would satisfy a partnership of individuals and allow for ownership and investment. The document that satisfied my needs is a **private placement memorandum**, or PPM.

This is a common pathway to the world of alternatives. A PPM requires its participants to be "accredited." According to Federal regulations, to be considered accredited, you must earn at least $200,000 in annual income or $300,000 if combined with your spouse. Alternatively, you could have $1 million in net worth, excluding your primary residence, or a trust valued at $5 million. Any of the above criteria would qualify you as an accredited investor. Currently, only accredited investors are allowed to invest in privately held companies—in other words, companies that are not listed on the NYSE or NASDAQ.

The PPM allowed me to involve other like-minded professionals and pursue projects with more significant income potential while minimizing the risk for the overall enterprise and participants. Private investors, not bound together using a PPM, are just capital-looking for the best returns without any organization. The PPM allowed me to easily organize the effort to provide a more extensive group's income.

The history behind these laws goes back to 1933. After the stock market crash and the Great Depression, individual investors were routinely taken advantage of by get-rich-quick schemes in real estate and the stock market. Many of these schemes involved unregulated private investments. The government created the Securities and Exchange Commission (SEC) to create laws in response. One of the SEC's first laws was to prevent non-accredited investors from investing in these deals. It created laws so private investing was only accessible to wealthy investors or the type of investor who could theoretically handle the potential loss. That made much sense back then; however, the world has significantly changed since the '30s. Wall Street is plagued with issues and self-interest. The finance industry is a trillion-dollar machine that generates Wall Street profits and the downstream is billions and billions of dollars at the expense of you and me. Wall Street's objective is to make money for Wall Street, not you.

Alternatives are simply those vehicles that are not the traditional Wall Street route— private equity, energy, private credit, real estate, and venture capital, to name a few. Alternative investments have generated outsized returns for the world's most astute investors. Between 1986 and 2022, private equity has outperformed the S&P 500 by over five percentage points annually (9.2% compared to 14.28%). That's a 50%+greater return. Private credit, an alternative to bonds, has generated two to three times the income/yield. It is undeniable that smart money uses high-quality alternative investments as the engine for greater diversification and accelerated growth.[10]

The reason for this increasing gap seems to be an ever-growing correlation in our markets:

"Correlation measures how much investments move together in the same direction (positively correlated means they move in unison, while negatively correlated means the opposite). There are varying degrees of correlation, meaning they move together but not in complete lockstep. For example, stocks and bonds have generally been uncorrelated. It is helpful if bonds go up to protect you when stocks go down. However, correlations are always changing and can often throw some unexpected curveballs. In 2022, stocks and bonds both dropped simultaneously. While this is somewhat rare, it may not be an anomaly. AQR, one of the world's most successful algorithmically driven hedge funds, believes that "macroeconomic changes—such as higher inflation

10   Costa, Moriah. "Private or Public: Investing in Private Credit vs Bonds." Money Made. (Oct 18, 2022.) Accessed (Mar 27, 2025). https://moneymade.io/learn/article/private-credit-vs-bonds

uncertainty—could lead to a reappearance of the positive stock-bond correlation of the 1970s, '80s, and '90s."[11]

In August 2023, a Bloomberg article read, "Bonds are a useless hedge for stock losses as correlation jumps." The article noted that the positive correlation between treasury bonds and stocks is at its highest since 1996!

For decades, the time-tested strategy for most ordinary investors has been the 60/40 portfolio (60% stocks, 40% bonds). Aside from providing income or yield, bonds have historically cushioned a portfolio in years when stocks are down. More recently, trends have consistently emerged; as referenced above, in 2022, the cushion was yanked out from under investors, and they landed flat on their behinds. Stocks and bonds both plummeted as interest rates rose and the economy began to slow down. Stocks and bonds moving in lockstep, also known as correlation, is precisely what you *don't* want in bear markets. 2022 was the first year in history when stocks and bonds dropped by the same magnitude (-22% annualized by October 31, 2022). The seven largest stocks in the S&P 500 went down an average of 46%. Put it all together, the 60/40 strategy experienced one of its worst performances in nearly a hundred years.[12] Since then, stocks and bonds have become even more correlated, not less. Bloomberg reported that "bonds are a useless hedge for stock losses as correlation jumps."

The problem is that today, most traditional diversification strategies and advisors tend to involve adding more and more

---

11   Xie, Ye. "Bonds Are Useless Hedge for Stock Losses as Correlation Jumps." Bloomberg. (Aug 2, 2023.) Accessed (Mar 27, 2025). https://www.bloomberg.com/news/articles/2023-08-02/bonds-are-useless-hedge-for-stock-losses-as-correlation-jumps

12   Whale Wisdom. Accessed (Mar 27, 2025). https://whalewisdom.com/filer/bridgewater-associates-inc

positively correlated investments. Many investors, knowingly or not, have given up on finding uncorrelated investments to help manage big swings. This abandonment of diversification is a high-stakes roll of the dice, but unfortunately, many Americans feel they have no choice or, worse yet, do not know the difference.

Alternatives in a portfolio can significantly assist in uncorrelated (or non-correlated) investments, which can dramatically reduce risk without sacrificing returns. Ray Dalio, founder of Bridgewater and one of the world's greatest alternative investors, demonstrates that a portfolio structured this way can minimize risk by as much as 80% while maintaining the same or similar upside potential. In 2008, while the market dropped 37%, Bridgewater alternatives bucked all trends and gave its investors a gain of 9.4%.[13,14]

To underscore this change in investing and the alternative landscape that is shifting, in 2006, approximately $1 trillion was being managed by private equity managers. Today, more than $6 trillion is allocated to private equity, with projections that the market will grow to more than $14 trillion by 2025. This "Great Migration" to alternatives seems unstoppable as the smart money is re-allocating. Fewer public equities, more private equity. Less public credit (bonds), more private credit. Fewer public REITs, more private real estate. According to the Financial Times, "The number of publicly traded U.S. companies has fallen by nearly half, to around forty-four hundred, since the peak

---

13   Whale Wisdom. Accessed (Mar 27, 2025). https://whalewisdom.com/filer/bridgewater-associates-inc

14   Mandl, Carolina. "Bridgewater's flagship fund posts gains of 32% through June." Reuters. (Jul 5, 2022.) Accessed (Mar 27, 2025). https://www.reuters.com/business/finance/bridgewaters-flagship-fund-posts-gains-32-through-june-2022-07-05/#:~:text=In%20the%20first%20half%20of%202022%2C%20the%20S%26P%20500%20was,an%20average%20of%2011.4%25%20annually

in 1996.[15] That's just forty-four hundred companies for investors to consider, and we all know many of them are mediocre at best regarding profitability, growth, and prospects. In 2009, 81% of public companies were profitable (post IPO); by 2021, only 28% (post IPO)."[16]

"When you look at the total value of all publicly traded companies globally, you may be shocked to learn that the value of all companies held by private equity funds dwarfs public stocks by nearly 4 to 1! Numerous studies have shown that adding private equity to a typical stock-and-bond portfolio reduces volatility and increases returns."[17,18]

15 "US Has Fewer Public Listed Companies Than China." Financial Times. Accessed (Mar 27, 2025). https://www.ft.com/content/73aa5bce-e433-11e9-9743-db5a370481bc

16 "Share of companies that were profitable after their IPO in the United States from 2005 to 2023." Statista. Accessed (Mar 27, 2025). https://www.statista.com/statistics/914724/profitable-companies-after-ipo-usa/

17 Prequin: World Federation of Exchanges

18 Tutrone, Anthony D. "Private Equity and Your Portfolio." Neuberger Berman. (Jan 2019.) Accessed (Mar 27, 2025). https://www.nb.com/en/global/insights/investment-quarterly-asset-matters-private-equity-and-your-portfolio

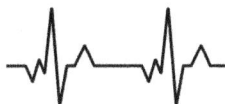

LEVERAGING TAX: MY
CHOSEN DIRECTION

Here's an example of a common mistake: After finishing residency, a physician partner was moving intensely into his financial future. He was aggressive in finding ways to reduce taxes and create cash flow. He had spent several years amassing single-family homes that were doing well. Still, he made a significant and common mistake—he fell into the trap of possessions, misunderstanding what true freedom means. He decided that since he had extra monthly income, he deserved a lake home and a boat! He placed a small down payment on a lake lot and purchased a used boat. He made payments utilizing a portion of his new-found cash flow. Soon followed the realization that he did not use the house as much as he and his family had imagined they would. Smart money says he would have been better off renting a lake house in an exotic location with the money it costs to service that real estate's debt.

He sold the lake house a few years later, but the money lost was the tuition paid for a valuable lesson.

In Talk #1, we asked, "Where do I want to be?" We encouraged taking stock and determining your desired lifestyle. This book is about generating the income needed to achieve financial freedom. If the goal is to own a vacation home on a lake, then build the cash-flow machine to support the second home *and* the time to enjoy it.

This talk is all about keeping the cash-flow machine working. What are some ways that your money can work harder for you? This is the core. Earlier talks focused on passive income's impact on your future Terminal Value Objective—how to build and maintain the machine to drive additional revenue. This talk takes it to the next level and discusses the other ways owning equity can positively impact your net worth.

DEBT: A MISUNDERSTOOD KEY TO CREATING FREEDOM

Contrary to what you may have been told growing up, not all debt is bad. Interest rates until recently have been at historic lows for years, and learning to harness the power of debt can create massive wealth. However, one personal and powerful rule in using debt is that you should only use it to buy assets, never liabilities. It is imperative to understand the difference.

Put more simply, the debt must be paid for by revenue from the asset. Even better is non-recourse debt. This is when the bank is your partner in the asset rather than strictly your debtor. For example, if you were to buy a rental home or duplex, you would place debt on the asset to increase your returns and, therefore, your leverage. However, this type of debt is considered recourse, meaning you are ultimately liable for the note if something happens. In non-recourse debt, the bank or lending institution is your partner, and the purchase's underwriting must qualify for the asset to stand alone on its cash flow and merits.

In this case, if the asset underperforms, you are not liable on your balance sheet. This type of transaction can lead to the ability to leverage millions of dollars and is ultimately how most successful entrepreneurs create wealth. There are many positives with non-recourse debt and the purchase of assets, but you must always consider your exit strategy first and know your timelines.

Using variable-rate debt products or bridge loans can be disastrous if you are not well-seasoned using these tools. **Always match the tool to the exit or goal.** One of the desirable aspects of using both real estate and oil and gas investments is that **real estate is typically always leveraged** in investments. In contrast, **many oil and gas assets seldom use debt, providing a balance and hedge to interest rate volatility.** This uncoupling or uncorrelating of your investing helps to balance a portfolio, which is why I chose this direction.

There is good debt and bad debt. Good debt is business loans, inventory loans, or loans on commercial buildings. Bad debt is expensive cars you can't afford, vacations on credit cards, or store cards for bags and shoes. Try to accumulate only good debt. The anecdote is this: **Bankers call you sir or ma'am whether you have a million dollars in the bank or owe a million dollars to the bank. Both are equally valuable to them.**

Physicians, like other highly compensated individuals, are prone to buying liabilities. They reward themselves with nice things from all the delayed gratification for all the time spent living under loans. In retrospect, this only increases expenses and further decreases the ability to create freedom. I am not advocating a life of frugality; on the contrary, it's OK to buy liabilities—but pay with cash. Use leverage and banking to purchase assets that will provide a payback.

TAXES REVISITED: THE LESS YOU PAY, THE MORE YOU KEEP

Most people don't find taxes sexy, but I do! For our physician investors, understanding and leveraging tax advantages has had the single most significant impact on personal wealth. Given this, I have learned to understand this topic very well. The single largest expense in many people's lives is taxes, and paying more than is required is insane, especially when it's avoidable. Failing to address tax implications can have a catastrophic impact on your portfolio. We touched on this concept earlier; however, Tony Robbins gives a great example in his book, *Unshakeable*: "Let's say you invest in a fund in December. Then, the next day, the manager sells the stock that has shot up over the past ten months. Since you're now an owner of the fund, you'll be getting a tax bill for those gains, even though you didn't benefit one bit from the stock's meteoric rise! Another common problem has to do with trading. Most funds constantly trade companies, selling off companies in the portfolio in less than a year. This means you will no longer benefit from lower capital gains taxes. Therefore, regardless of how long you hold the fund, you'll be taxed at your physician capital gains rates!"

The lesson is to learn to invest in income-producing assets that offset and decrease tax burdens. A doctor's greatest assets are knowledge, experience, and earning power. Leverage that gift positively. That's great for all the years of sacrifice we have undertaken to serve our calling as healthcare providers. Unfortunately, with significant income also comes substantial tax bills.

Have you ever wondered how your neighbors who own small companies or who are developers or home builders seem to do so well? The answer is the miracle of ownership. The government dramatically incentivizes owners, job creators, and those segments that are important to the economy and that the government cannot provide on its own. A physician's income will likely dwarf many investors' incomes; however, the investor will pay a fraction of the tax paid by an average physician.

Physicians are often taxed at the highest level, with no assets to offset the income. Investors and owners, for example, have significant equity position assets, which can provide depreciation losses that significantly reduce the taxes they pay, boosting their earnings. Oil and gas investments also have some of the most significant tax incentives and write-offs. Intangible Drilling Costs (IDCs) can write off vast portions of invested funds, and portions of profits can be exempted from taxes! Our goal is to create passive income while reducing the tax basis. Writing off a stethoscope and a few pairs of scrubs at the end of the year will never get you to the level needed for lasting wealth and cash flow.

MY TWO CHOSEN ALTERNATIVE DIRECTIONS

Real Estate & Depreciation

Real estate is the undisputed king of alternative investments and is the oldest and largest asset class. It is likely a part of most successful investor portfolios in some fashion, whether a single-family rental, ownership in a multifamily apartment property, or both. With 7.9 billion people on earth, residential real estate is naturally the largest category, with a global value of $258 trillion! Everyone needs a place to live, regardless of the economy and interest rates. North America alone represents nearly 20% of the world's total real estate value despite holding just 7% of the world's population.[10]

There are numerous real estate subcategories, from self-storage and industrial to hotels. I have owned many of them. Over many decades, real estate performance has generated conservative mid-single-digit to low-double-digit returns. But leverage has allowed for substantially higher returns and considerably higher risk! Of course, returns depend on location, the local economy, the amount of leverage (loan-to-value levels), and nu-

---

10 Tostevin, Paul. "The total value of global real estate." Savills. (Sep 2021.) Accessed (Mar 27, 2025). https://www.savills.com/impacts/market-trends/the-total-value-of-global-real-estate.html

merous other factors. Real estate is also an asset class that, for U.S. investors, offers government-sanctioned tax avoidance. As a refresher, taxpaying real estate investors benefit from "depreciation," which means the cash flows from real estate income can often be sheltered from some or all taxation.

Depreciation is the decline in the value of an asset over time. For example, a new vehicle purchase depreciates when driven off the lot. Just try to trade it within a month of purchase, and you'll understand depreciation quite well. Though depreciation implies a loss, real estate investing is positive regarding income. Real estate depreciates. Toilets, sinks, roofs, and all real estate investment items are depreciable except the land (Land is a fixed cost and does not depreciate). Tax laws allow the asset owner to deduct the structure's depreciation. This is a critical concept in real estate investing. The value of a real estate investment, such as an apartment complex, can appreciate over time, thus creating more equity for the owner, while the value of the building depreciates, reducing its tax basis. This, in turn, reduces the taxes paid on the assets that are appreciating simultaneously.

Read my article in *Forbes*: "Why Depreciation is the Biggest Perk of Real Estate Investing"

Also, investors can avoid paying taxes on any increase in value when their property is sold by exercising the option of buying more property and rolling over the gains as equity in the new investment. This is called a 1031 exchange. Done repeatedly, this can create a perpetual deferral of taxation. To take it a step further, some investors can eliminate taxes on ALL their accumulated gains with clever and entirely legal estate planning (particularly in the U.S.). Many of the preeminent real estate families know this tactic quite well.

Real estate has been the cornerstone of wealth for centuries. Everything in investing runs in cycles, and you will always make the money on the buy, not the sell. As of 2022, we have entered a time when interest rates are changing, and the laws of supply and demand are in flux. There are always opportunities around if you have the experience and relationships. In the changing cycle, things can be harder or easier based on the period. Be patient and be persistent!

OIL & GAS AND INTANGIBLE DRILLING COSTS (IDCS)

The story of human progress is a story of energy. Before our ability to harness energy efficiently, we lived brutally short lives of survival. We hunted, gathered, and lit fires to keep us warm and cook our food. This was our way of life for millennia. Aside from the elites, the vast majority were poor, illiterate, uneducated, diseased, and malnourished. Both then and now, these are the plagues of a population without energy.

We are experiencing an energy revolution wherein renewable sources of clean(er) energy are evolving from less clean energy sources. This trend will continue, but according to numerous experts, traditional fossil fuels will likely never be entirely replaced. This might be a shock if you thought society would flip a switch and rid itself of fossil fuels. This certainly sounds like the case when renewables are discussed in the media. However, the likely outcome is that technological innovation will make existing fossil fuels much cleaner and greener. Technologies that can do just what already exists will take time to scale.

Around 2010, society began moving toward wind, solar, and

other renewables. Today, after *thirteen years and nearly $1 trillion invested*, these renewable sources provide just 3% of the world's energy needs. Given the choice, we all want cleaner forms of energy, and we can surely get there with innovation. However, we must also understand how long new sources take to gain substantial market share. If you are reading this, you realize that this equates to opportunity.

In investing, we must separate the facts from our feelings. Hearing "energy transition," one might naturally think we are switching from fossil fuels to renewables. Nothing could be further from the truth. Modern man has always been "transitioning" to different forms of energy, which is why the word "transition" is an unfortunate misnomer. Wil VanLoh is the founder of Quantum Energy Partners, one of the largest private energy investors in the world. He believes that energy "addition" would be a more apt term. Why? VanLoh explains that when we look at history, we can see that it takes a very long time for new energy sources to be adopted and that they have never entirely replaced the previously dominant forms of energy. He laid out the data showing we are undergoing modern history's fifth energy addition/transition.

"In the early 1900s, following the production of Henry Ford's first Model T, we began transitioning from coal to oil. It took fifty years for oil to reach 25% of global energy market share. In 2023, we are on track to use more oil than any year in history, with 2024 projected to be even higher."[11,12]

---

11   Lawler, Alex. "OPEC sees 2.2% oil demand growth in 2024 despite headwinds." Reuters. (Jul 13, 2023.) Accessed (Mar 27, 2025). https://www.reuters.com/business/energy/opec-upbeat-over-2024-oil-demand-outlook-despite-headwinds-2023-07-13/

12   "Gas 2020." IEA. (2020.) Accessed (Mar 27, 2025). https://www.iea.org/reports/gas-2020/2021-2025-rebound-and-beyond

When we look at the future, experts foresee two unavoidable variables impacting energy demand. **The first variable is population growth**—the global population has grown from 2.5 billion in 1950 to more than 8 billion today. The International Monetary Fund (IMF) predicts that the global population will continue to surge, reaching 9.7 billion by 2050.[13] As the world marches forward, a combination of technology, advances in healthcare, and access to energy will propel the world's billions from relative poverty into the middle class. Just look back to a relatively short time ago in China and India. Population explosions and development are changing the face of global demand. People who earn more spend more, and they undoubtedly use more energy. The point is, we aren't dealing with a static amount of energy usage; we are dealing with the ever-increasing demand. The world's population currently uses about 100 million barrels of oil daily, which is only expected to grow. By 2050, most experts believe the global energy demand will increase by roughly 50%. This is a reasonable estimate considering demand grew by 50% between 1990 and 2020.

The second variable is one of constraint—a depleting supply. If you ask one hundred people who is the largest energy producer in the world, many will say Saudi Arabia. But they would be wrong. The United States is the world's largest oil and gas producer. We produce about 22% of the world's supply, with Russia (15%) and Saudi Arabia (9%) in second and third place.[14] Not only are we the largest, but we are also the cleanest (rela-

---

13 "Oil company Phillips 66 says it will shut down Los Angeles-area refinery." AP News. (Oct 16, 2024.) Accessed (Mar 27, 2025). https://apnews.com/article/california-refinery-oil-phillips-66-shut-down-bbea1826c0d5d472273f97ad86b870f8

14 Peterson, Kimberly; Russo, Jonathan. "China increased electricity generation annually from 2000 to 2020." U.S. Energy Information Administration. (Sep 22, 2022.) Accessed (Mar 27, 2025). https://www.eia.gov/todayinenergy/detail.php?id=53959

tively speaking). Case in point, U.S. natural gas is about 30% cleaner than Russian natural gas.[15] Besides working to generate the cleanest versions of our fossil fuels, our energy independence and standing as the world's largest producer gives us tremendous economic, food, and national security advantages.

The world's energy use shakes to about 100 million barrels (or barrel equivalents) daily. To put that into perspective, a football stadium would hold about 2 million barrels. That total use equates to fifty football stadiums' worth of oil *every day*. That adds up to 36.5 billion barrels yearly to keep our world's economic engine running. Population growth and economic expansion mean demand is expected to grow by 1–2% per year, or 365–700 million barrels. But how much do we deplete the existing supply each year? This is the trillion-dollar question. The global "supply decline rate" is 7–8% annually. This means that existing fossil fuel reservoirs and deposits are losing 7–8% of their total finite capacity per year. That's 7–8 million barrels of daily supply that we need to replace *each and every* year just to keep pace with current demand, not to mention attempting to meet the market's future growth. This is the equivalent of finding 3-4 new United States' worth of energy production in the next 20 years.

As mentioned earlier, the government incentivizes investors to provide things the economy needs that it cannot do. Domestic oil and gas remain among the best tax-advantaged alternative investment opportunities available, and long-term economics only point to massive demand versus supply side shifts to the investor. Similar to real estate, energy commodities run in cycles.

---

15 "John Kerry Tilts at Chinese Coal Plants." *The Wall Street Journal*. (Jul 17, 2023.) Accessed (Mar 27, 2025). https://www.wsj.com/articles/john-kerry-china-climate-economy-xi-jinping-beijing-e50b9ef4?mod=hp_trending_now_opn_pos1

These peaks and troughs tend to be uncorrelated, which is why I like the asset (in addition to the massive tax benefits). Geopolitical issues and inflation tend to improve this investment, and we are indeed in a changing world.

By investing in these assets, Accredited Investors unlock various potential incentives, including deductions for exploration costs and a lower taxable income, thereby reducing their overall tax liabilities. Specifically, Intangible Drilling Costs (IDCs) are expenses related to developing an oil or gas well that are not a part of the final operating well. They include costs for drilling and preparing wells to produce oil and gas, such as survey work, ground clearing, drainage, wages, fuel, repairs, and supplies. These are extremely powerful in offsetting tax liabilities in other investment ventures and W2 income!

Two of ten prior Blackbridge Financial Triple net (NNN) holdings in Kilgore, Texas, oil field area of operations.

The roots of our company, Blackbridge Financial, first began over a decade ago at the intersection of real estate depreciation and oil field operations. Our history in the East Texas oil field spans to our company beginnings. We have owned numerous triple-net industrial warehouse assets, forging partners in the oil and gas industry. From wellhead manufacturers to wire cable lifting and drilling products, our roots have cultivated the relationships that have led us to our current investment structure!

SECRETS

- Tax reduction is the lubricant and the incentive—it levers or speeds the machine up.
- Make the banker your partner; there is an excellent opportunity in non-recourse debt.
- Understanding the value of depreciation and IDCs will help you refine your strategy. Taking advantage of these powerful tools is the key to passive income.
- Oil and gas opportunities are some of the most lucrative and tax-efficient ways of creating wealth. New structures have eliminated risks in joint partnerships, and we are at the forefront of a paradigm shift in investing.

CHECKLIST

- ☐ Evaluate your current debt load and create a plan to convert your bad debt into good debt as you progress through your investment strategy.
- ☐ Assemble your tax package and find a tax professional who can guide you through the benefits of tax-sheltering and tax-incentivized investments.
- ☐ Go to www.blackbridge.financial/education for more learning opportunities. We have developed a brief course outlining the specifics of this asset and the unique golden age we

are approaching.

THE FINAL THOUGHT: USING YOUR GREATEST ASSET

A high-earning power is a massive investment advantage, allowing you to leverage yourself to freedom and wealth. You are accredited and you have grit. It took grit, as well as passion and intellect, to become a doctor. As a physician, you are usually part of a more extensive network of like-minded physicians and technical experts, people with knowledge and cash flow who are looking for opportunities. Developing and using this network will become substantial over time. Investing is a team sport, and your network is critical. As we discovered in Talk #3, your future comes from your network. Each member of your team has a role to play.

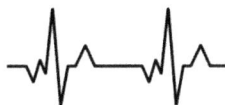

CLOSING

I walked away from the Navy in 1998. The destroyer I had spent four years on, including three overseas deployments, was being decommissioned. It was bittersweet, but I was ready to tackle the next phase of my life. I had been saving for years for my formal education; that, along with my GI bill, allowed me to plan for my education. Once back home, I sought a financial advisor with a well-known national advisory group. I had no formal financial education and fell prey to the message that they had my best interests in mind.

For over a decade, I was a small client, yet every time I made an appointment, I was treated like I was important and mattered. Years later, after undergrad and medical school, my income increased, and I invested more considerable sums, continuing to enjoy the same fantastic treatment. My financial advisor appeared to be my friend. For years, I made the maximum contribution to my IRA. As I became more educated and took a more active role in my finances and investment strategy, I realized that fees affected my returns. I needed help finding an accurate cost basis for my statements. How could just a few hundred thousand dollars generate twenty pages of statements and endless footnotes?

My irritation with conventional investing and my love for alternative investments and tax benefits collided, and my strategy changed. Like medicine, real estate was more "evidence-based," and I could predict the outcome of an investment with statistical accuracy rather than throwing dice or praying my advisor understood each fund he was selling. To my financial advisor's shock, I made a big move and removed all my money from the market. I felt guilty, almost like I was losing a friend.

I had an epiphany numerous years later. My daughter and I were shopping at a local grocery store when I ran into my former financial advisor. He was slightly behind me in stride when I opened the door. Our eyes met, and he said thanks; to my shock, he had no idea who I was. I was a dutiful customer for fifteen years. He celebrated my marriage and my children's births via greeting cards; we connected a few times a year. But there was an unmistakable blank look on his face. He had no clue who I was. Not even a second glance when I politely stalked him, "bumping" into him at the register. I felt betrayed but somehow profoundly relieved. However, I soon realized his career was like mine because we talked daily to numerous customers and patients. I strive to give the best experience possible, but I too am guilty of not knowing all of my patients well, especially if I see them only two or three times per year. I will never see financial advisors the same again. Many of them are great people, and I respect their practices. I'm just suggesting that you use your skill as a physician to think about the alternatives; you will see the world as I began seeing it. The machine was mine to build. I had the solution, the ideas, and a dream to pursue.

TAKING CARE OF YOU

Aside from owning the practice, the reality is that most of us are employees somehow, whether to ourselves or to a group. We make money only for what we do. If I don't show up, if I am sick or injured or on vacation, I don't generate income. So, aside from owning a practice, we each need to work to develop an investment strategy that generates passive income. We need to build that machine that continues to create wealth and help us meet our Terminal Value Objective.

We and the hundreds of physicians who trust and invest with us believe that the "alternative" space is the best vehicle to generate income. It is tangible and limited, uses leverage in multiple ways, and provides a lucrative tax advantage when needed.

THE END GAME

We all began in medicine for a reason, and I would bet that for many of you, it was using your love of science to help people. However, one cannot ignore that the *business of medicine* is rampant with cloaked truths and driven by money. How many drugs are created year after year treating one condition, to be used "off market" for others? How often have we seen a drug that is no longer patented combined with another to create a new drug for the same condition, magically producing a new product and a litany of new commercials?

Billboards scatter the landscape: "I am thankful to be alive since 'Hospital X' saved my life. Number 1 in Patient Care!" Why do healthcare systems place ads like this? We all know the answer: revenue. If there were no revenue behind it, there would be no sign. Nonprofit hospitals have enormous tax breaks, and they stockpile cash. Insurance companies are making record profits in the billions. Healthcare mandates have lessened the number of insured. Burnout among physicians has reached epidemic levels, and we wonder why this is. Medicine and money are evil juxtaposed twins. By navigating the endless documentation requirements in an EMR and losing patient interaction, we have ceased to be a profession for the patients. We have lost our way. We order tests but over-order to satiate our legal defenses and satisfy our patients in the current "I want it now" society.

My "ask" of you who are reading this:

☐ Keep this with you, and remember that all your sacrifices will ultimately lead you to where you want to be.

☐ We cannot change the healthcare landscape, but we can change how we live, earn, and prosper to accommodate the environment.

☐ Share these words with at least three of your colleagues. We can all find success together.

☐ Visit www.blackbridge.financial for more learning opportunities.

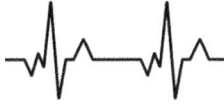

ABOUT THE AUTHOR

Dr. Thomas Black, MD MBA is an accomplished physician, veteran, and investing professional. His most recent venture, a physician-based investment company, executed over $1 billion in transactions, specializing in acquiring, managing, and operating alternative assets. The company was a three-time selectee for the INC 5000's Fastest Growing Companies in the *US Magazine* in 2020, 2021, and 2022 and was named a Top 100 Company by *Fort Worth Business Press* in 2020 and 2021. In 2021, Tom was awarded as one of *Fort Worth Magazine's* annual "Top Entrepreneurs of the Year" and has been featured in *Forbes Magazine* as a contributor.

Tom served in the Navy, Army, and Air Force while in the armed forces. He then earned his medical degree from the University of Texas Medical Branch, where he was selected as a member of the Alpha Omega Alpha Medical Honor Society and a Magna Cum laude graduate of the honors in research program. After completing his medical degree, he completed his post-doctoral residency training in Emergency Medicine at the University of Indiana and an MBA from the University of Tennessee at Knoxville. After being in private practice for several years, from his partnership due to a growing private equity involvement in healthcare. This led to creating platforms designed around physician access to private alternative investments.

Tom brings his passion for educating others about leveraging investments to maximize personal net worth and build a path to financial freedom. He has published several books, most recently *The Tax Cure*, which details his successful financial path to a life outside of medicine. Although no longer clinically working, Tom remains a board-certified emergency physician to fuel his passion for helping others find financial success.

WORKS CITED

Costa, Moriah. "Private or Public: Investing in Private Credit vs Bonds." Money Made. (Oct 18, 2022.) Accessed (Mar 27, 2025). https://moneymade.io/learn/article/private-credit-vs-bonds

Xie, Ye. "Bonds Are Useless Hedge for Stock Losses as Correlation Jumps." Bloomberg. (Aug 2, 2023.) Accessed (Mar 27, 2025). https://www.bloomberg.com/news/articles/2023-08-02/bonds-are-useless-hedge-for-stock-losses-as-correlation-jumps

Whale Wisdom. Accessed (Mar 27, 2025). https://whalewisdom.com/filer/bridgewater-associates-inc

"US Has Fewer Public Listed Companies Than China." Financial Times. Accessed (Mar 27, 2025). https://www.ft.com/content/73aa5bce-e433-11e9-9743-db5a370481bc

"Share of companies that were profitable after their IPO in the United States from 2005 to 2023 ." Statista. Accessed (Mar 27, 2025). https://www.statista.com/statistics/914724/profitable-companies-after-ipo-usa/

Mandl, Carolina. "Bridgewater's flagship fund posts gains of 32% through June." Reuters. (Jul 5, 2022.) Accessed (Mar 27, 2025). https://www.reuters.com/business/finance/bridgewaters-flagship-fund-posts-gains-32-through-june-2022-07-05/#:~:text=In%20the%20first%20half%20of%202022%2C%20the%20S%26P%20500%20was,an%20average%20of%2011.4%25%20annually

Prequin: World Federation of Exchanges. Accessed (Mar 27, 2025). https://www.preqin.com/

Tutrone, Anthony D. "Private Equity and Your Portfolio." Neuberger Berman. (Jan 2019.) Accessed (Mar 27, 2025). https://www.nb.com/en/global/insights/investment-quarterly-asset-matters-private-equity-and-your-portfolio

Peterson, Kimberly; Russo, Jonathan. "China increased electricity generation annually from 2000 to 2020." U.S. Energy Information Administration. (Sep 22, 2022.) Accessed (Mar 27, 2025). https://www.eia.gov/todayinenergy/detail.php?id=53959

"John Kerry Tilts at Chinese Coal Plants." The Wall Street Journal. (Jul 17, 2023.) Accessed (Mar 27, 2025). https://www.wsj.com/articles/john-kerry-china-climate-economy-xi-jinping-beijing-e50b9ef4?mod=hp_trending_now_opn_pos1

Surran, Carl. "No new refineries likely ever built again in the U.S., Chevron CEO warns." Seeking Alpha. (Jun 3, 2022.) Accessed (Mar 27, 2025). https://seekingalpha.com/news/3845705-no-new-refineries-likely-ever-built-again-in-the-us-chevron-ceo-warns

Lawler, Alex. "OPEC sees 2.2% oil demand growth in 2024 despite headwinds." Reuters. (Jul 13, 2023.) Accessed (Mar 27, 2025). https://www.reuters.com/business/energy/opec-upbeat-over-2024-oil-demand-outlook-despite-headwinds-2023-07-13/

"Gas 2020." IEA. (2020.) Accessed (Mar 27, 2025). https://www.iea.org/reports/gas-2020/2021-2025-rebound-and-beyond

Ruiz, Neil; Noe-Bustamante, Luis; Saber, Nadya. "Coming of Age." International Monetary Fund. (Mar 2020.) Accessed (Mar 27, 2025). https://www.imf.org/en/

Publications/fandd/issues/2020/03/infographic-global-population-trends-picture

"Oil company Phillips 66 says it will shut down Los Angeles-area refinery." AP News. (Oct 16, 2024.) Accessed (Mar 27, 2025). https://apnews.com/article/california-refinery-oil-phillips-66-shut-down-bbea1826c0d5d472273f9 7ad86b870f8

Tostevin, Paul. "The total value of global real estate." Savills. (Sep 2021.) Accessed (Mar 27, 2025). https://www.savills. com/impacts/market-trends/the-total-value-of-global-real-estate.html